THE WHO
FOR CLASSICAL PIANO

15 OF THEIR BEST ARRANGED BY PHILLIP KEVEREN

```
— PIANO LEVEL —
INTERMEDIATE
```

ISBN: 978-1-5400-2997-3

Visit Hal Leonard Online at
www.halleonard.com

Visit Phillip at
www.phillipkeveren.com

Contact us:
Hal Leonard
7777 West Bluemound Road
Milwaukee, WI 53213
Email: info@halleonard.com

In Europe, contact:
Hal Leonard Europe Limited
42 Wigmore Street
Marylebone, London, W1U 2RN
Email: info@halleonardeurope.com

In Australia, contact:
Hal Leonard Australia Pty. Ltd.
4 Lentara Court
Cheltenham, Victoria, 3192 Australia
Email: info@halleonard.com.au

PREFACE

Formed in London in 1964, The Who are considered one of the most influential rock bands of the 20th century. Their songs cover a lot of stylistic ground, providing the arranger with rich material for interpretation.

For this arranger, "Pinball Wizard" carries the most memories – and it makes a fantastic romp at the piano! "I Can See for Miles," with its intriguing fluidity between major and minor modes, is a hauntingly beautiful piece of music. "The Kids Are Alright" provides a foray into more traditional classical fare.

As always, listening to the original recordings of the songs will be helpful in your interpretation of these classical settings.

Musically yours,

Phillip Keveren

Phillip Keveren

CONTENTS

BABA O'RILEY

Words and Music by
PETER TOWNSHEND
Arranged by Phillip Keveren

R.H. over L.H.

R.H. over L.H.

R.H. over L.H.

GOING MOBILE

Words and Music by
PETER TOWNSHEND
Arranged by Phillip Keveren

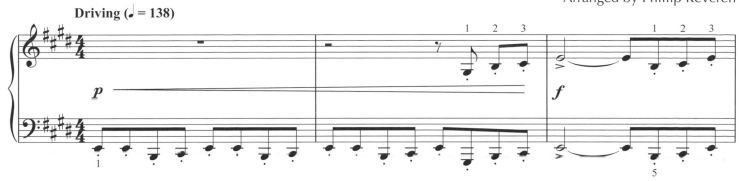

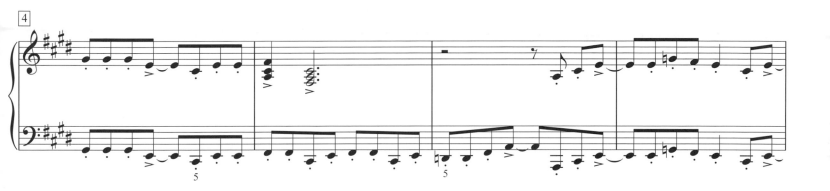

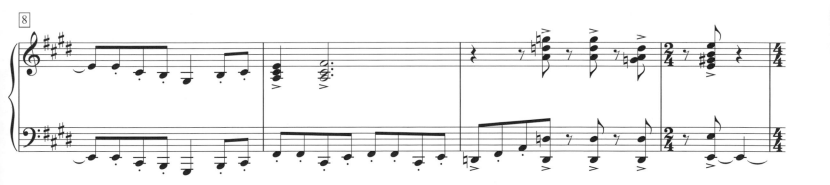

BARGAIN

Words and Music by
PETER TOWNSHEND
Arranged by Phillip Keveren

Flowing (♩ = 138)

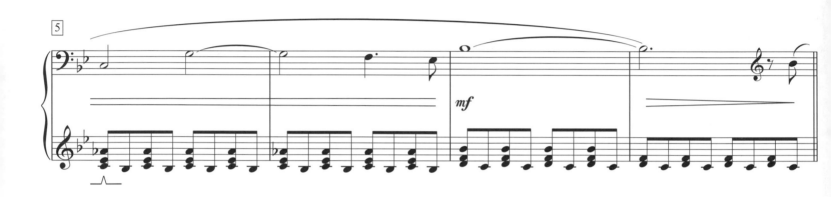

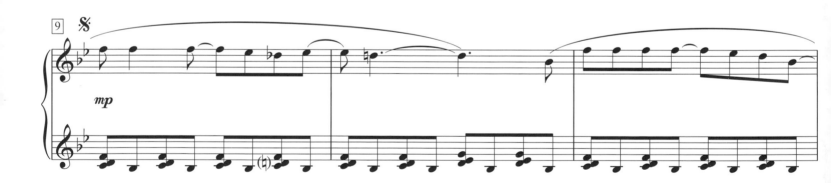

BEHIND BLUE EYES

Words and Music by
PETER TOWNSHEND
Arranged by Phillip Keveren

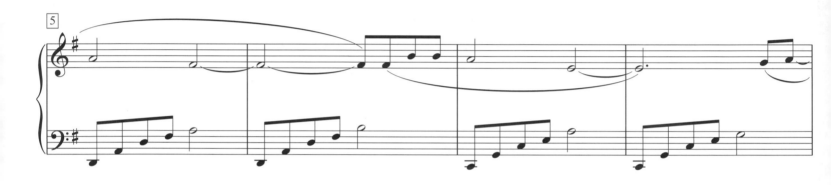

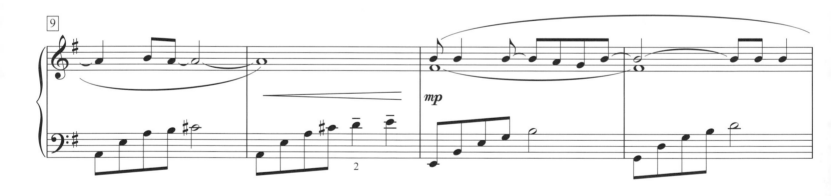

DON'T LET GO THE COAT

Words and Music by
PETER TOWNSHEND
Arranged by Phillip Keveren

I CAN SEE FOR MILES

Words and Music by
PETER TOWNSHEND
Arranged by Phillip Keveren

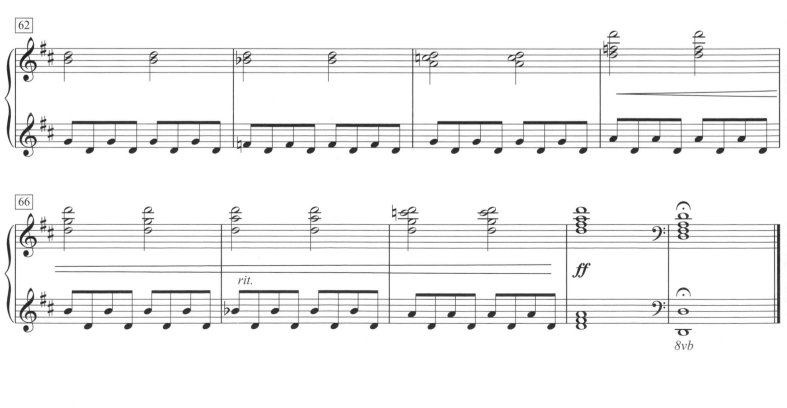

THE KIDS ARE ALRIGHT

Words and Music by
PETER TOWNSHEND
Arranged by Phillip Keveren

LOVE, REIGN O'ER ME

Words and Music by
PETER TOWNSHEND
Arranged by Phillip Keveren

THE MAGIC BUS

Words and Music by
PETER TOWNSHEND
Arranged by Phillip Keveren

SQUEEZE BOX

Words and Music by
PETER TOWNSHEND
Arranged by Phillip Keveren

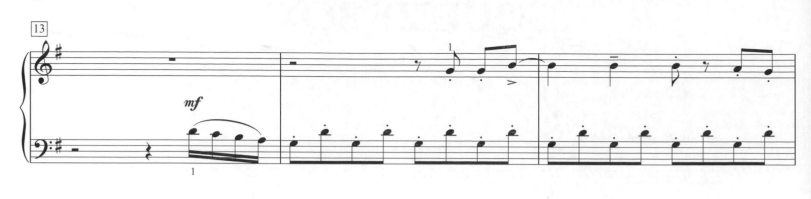

MY GENERATION

Words and Music by
PETER TOWNSHEND
Arranged by Phillip Keveren

PINBALL WIZARD

Words and Music by
PETER TOWNSHEND
Arranged by Phillip Keveren

WHO ARE YOU

Words and Music by
PETER TOWNSHEND
Arranged by Phillip Keveren

Flowing (♩ = 132–138)

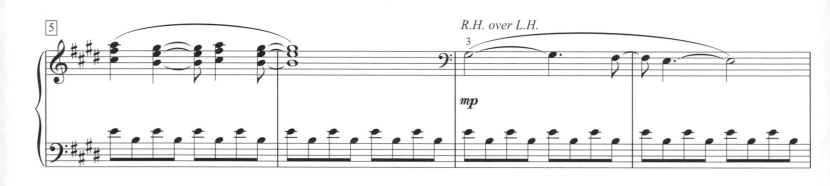

pp

Pedal liberally

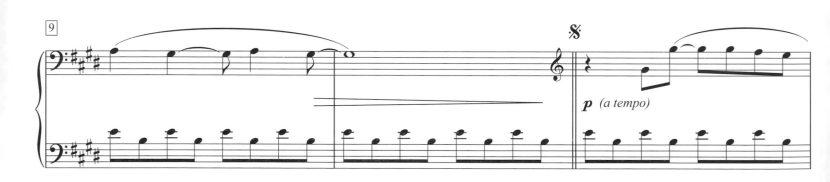

R.H. over L.H.

mp

p *(a tempo)*

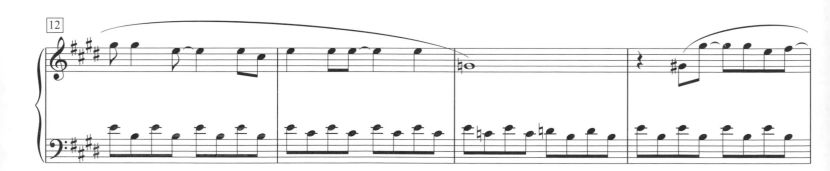

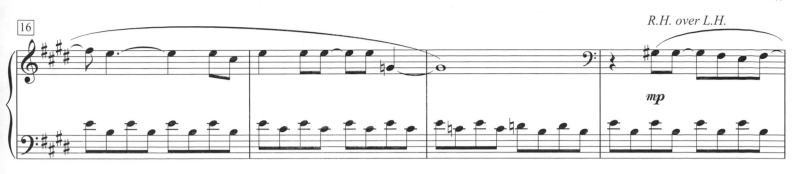

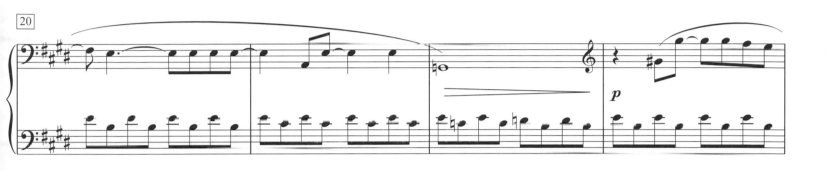

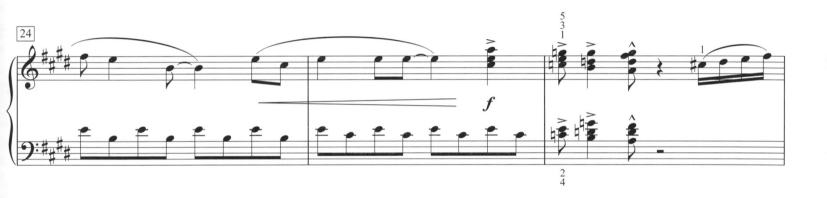

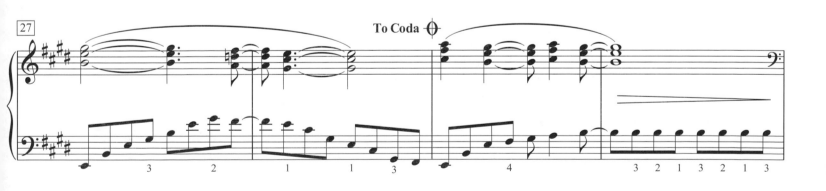

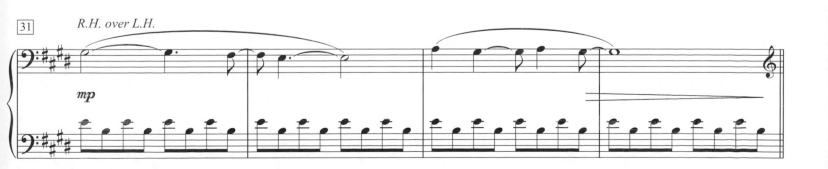

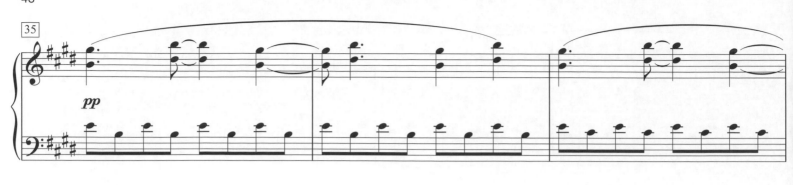

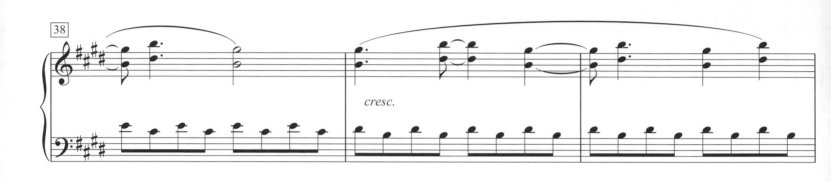

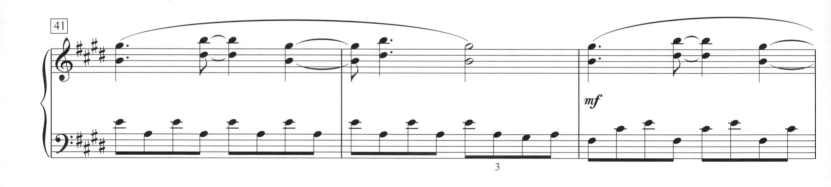

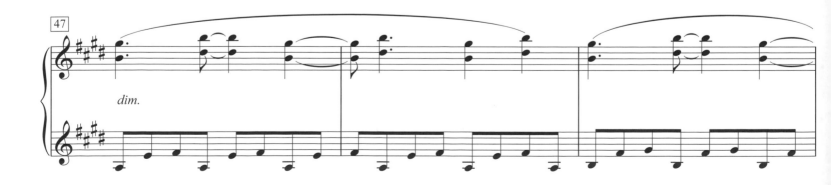

WON'T GET FOOLED AGAIN

Words and Music by
PETER TOWNSHEND
Arranged by Phillip Keveren

YOU BETTER YOU BET

Words and Music by
PETER TOWNSHEND
Arranged by Phillip Keveren